IS GOD FOR REAL?

Answers to Five Common Myths about God, Jesus, and the Bible

MICHAEL GREEN AND GORDON CARKNER

BARBOUR
PUBLISHING, INC.
Uhrichsville, Ohio

Published by Barbour Publishing, Inc., P. O. Box 719, Uhrichsville, Ohio 44683 http://www.barbourbooks.com

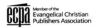

Member of the
Evangelical Christian
Publishers Association

Printed in the United States of America.

CONTENTS

INTRODUCTION

I t was the best of times: It was the worst of times." These words of Charles Dickens to describe the years of the French Revolution fit our own day remarkably well. Yes, it is the best of times: Would you prefer to have lived in any other century? The fantastic advances in science and technology, the control of disease and the length of life, the comfort of homes and the ease of travel in what has become a global village. . . It would all have been undreamed-of even a hundred years ago.

But it is no less the worst of times. There has never been such a threat to life on this planet as there is today. Never has there been such rape of our world's resources, never such famine, so many deaths by torture. The injustice in society, the breakdown of marriage, the abuse of wives and children, the absence of values, and the inhuman way we treat each other are breathtaking in a world that is considered civilized. The old Russian joke hits close to home: "Under capitalism man exploits man. Under communism the reverse is true"! Underneath all the surface ills of our society there is a profound loss of identity and purpose. Who am I? Where is the world going? What really matters? What will last? The old remedies for the human condition have been found wanting. The optimism of the humanists? Shattered on the rock of two bestial world wars and the continual carnage in world society. Marxism's economic restructuring? Human hearts remain as unfulfilled in China as in Manhattan. Materialism? Utterly selfish and utterly unsatisfying—some of the richest people in the world are the most unhappy. Dr. Ronald Conway, a leading Australian psychiatrist, wrote of Melbourne society what is true of many "first-world" countries: "We have in parts of Melbourne the highest barbiturate dependence in the world, the highest suicide rate among young males between eighteen and thirty, the highest declared rate of rape in the world, and one in four women and one in ten men are suffering from depression. Australians have everything, and yet they have nothing to live for." Where, then, shall we look for an answer to the most profound questions of our lives and our society? Is there any guidance to be had? Are there any values that will last?

During the height of the Roman Empire, at

the crossroads of Greek, Roman, and Jewish culture, Jesus of Nazareth was born. His life and teaching, His claim to be God, His death and resurrection have captured the hearts and minds of millions all over the world during the past two thousand years, and today a third of the world's population claims to follow Him.

Here was His Manifesto:

> "The Spirit of the Lord is on me,
> because he has anointed me to preach
> good news to the poor. He has sent me
> to proclaim freedom for the prisoners
> and recovery of sight for the blind, to
> release the oppressed, to proclaim the
> year of the Lord's favor" (Luke 4:18–19).

He claims that He has come to bring the answer to the human condition, reconcile the estranged, and bring hope to the most despairing. So immensely valuable are we to God that Jesus has come to show us what God is like and to call for our commitment. As we surrender ourselves to that undeserved love, we shall discover what life is all about and what human beings were made for. That is the claim, no less.

But is it credible that this individual from two thousand years ago can have anything to say to our modern world? Can today's rootless, emotionally wounded men and women find any reason for hope in Jesus of Nazareth? We believe they can. Many thousands of people every day across the world are entrusting their lives to this Jesus, most in Africa, Asia, and Latin America. Properly understood, and personally trusted, He remains the only hope for mankind—the only way to God.

But myths cluster around Jesus, God, and Bible like barnacles on the bottom of a ship after a long voyage. This book attempts to scrape off the barnacles, to explode the myths, and to enable you to make a considered response. The five myths we have chosen are not arbitrary. They represent what a great many people think and say. Because they insulate people from God, they need to be ripped away. If we are to accept Jesus as God, we need to be clear what we are accepting. If we reject Him, we need to be equally clear what it is we are rejecting and why. It is the aim of this little book to make the issues crystal clear.

ALL THE EVIL AND SUFFERING IN THE WORLD PROVES THERE IS NO GOD

Many people think that the problem of evil, with the suffering it brings, is an insuperable barrier to belief in a good God. The argument can be deployed like this:

- A God who is good and loving would not want to allow evil and suffering in His world.
- A God who is all-powerful could remove evil and suffering if He so desired.
- Therefore, if God is both good and powerful, there should be no evil or suffering.
- But undeniably there is evil and there is pain. So God (at least a good and powerful God) does not exist.

This argument is superficially impressive. But do those who ask for evil to be eradicated really think what they are asking? Just suppose for a moment that God were immediately to wipe out all evil. Where would we stand? Would not humanity be destroyed? For which of us is free from evil? Far from remaining an abstract, intellectual problem, evil is a very pressing moral problem within each one of us. We ourselves are the problem of evil. And if simple eradication were the answer, we would have no hope.

Or just suppose for a moment that the problem of pain and evil drives you to reject the existence of a loving God and to imagine that some monster rules our destiny or that the stars are in charge of our fortunes, how does that help? You may have gotten rid of one set of problems, but you have replaced them with a much bigger one. How do you explain kindness, goodness, love and humanity, unselfishness, and gentleness in a world that is governed by a horrible monster or by the uncaring stars? Because life is not all evil. It is far more complex than that.

On any showing, evil and pain in the world constitute a massive problem both to belief and to behavior. And Christianity offers no knock-down solution at a philosophical level. But the Bible does give us ground to stand on as we try to live in a world where suffering is real. Because it teaches us that God is no stranger to pain.

- The Bible teaches that God did not create evil and pain. The world He made was utterly good (Genesis 1:31). But as early as that marvelous pictorial story of Adam and Eve we find humanity turning against God, using His gift of free will to rebel. And that brought the perfection of God's world tumbling down. Somehow there is a profound link between mankind and his environment. When humanity fell out of step with God and His purposes, and moral evil entered the world through that rebellion, suffering came in as well. There cannot be evil without suffering. The Bible goes on to assert that behind human wickedness there lies a great outside influence, the devil, who hates God and everything to do with Him (John 8:44). Jesus taught often about the reality of this evil force, who is out to spoil both mankind and his environment and do everything possible to attack God and His purposes of good. The Bible makes it plain that somehow this malign force is involved in the evil and suffering of this world. There is a war on between the forces of good and evil, and we are all caught up in that war every day (Ephesians 6:10–18). Such is the biblical teaching. Does it not ring true?

- Again, the Bible teaches that although God did not create evil and suffering, and although He does not will it, nevertheless He can and does use it. The presence of evil in the world has led many to strive for good. The presence of suffering in the world has produced qualities of character that would have been impossible without it—courage, endurance, self-sacrifice, compassion. . . God uses pain in a profound way to draw us to Himself when normally we will not listen. In our pleasures He merely whispers. In our suffering He shouts.

- God did not leave us to stew in the mess we had made for ourselves. He became involved. He came to this world with all its sorrow and pain, its wickedness and entrenched evil (John 3:16–19). He came as a man among men. He lived in squalor and suffering. He knew thirst and hunger, flogging and heartbreak, fear and despair. He ended His life in one of the most excruciating of all deaths. So let nobody say that God does not care, and does not understand. He has personally gone through it all.

- God has dealt with the problem of evil and suffering at its root. Jesus not only shared our pain and agony on the cross (John 19:1–30), He took personal responsibility for the wickedness of every man or woman who has ever lived or ever will. He allowed that vast mountain of evil to crush Him. And it cost Him unspeakable suffering. It cost Him hell. He cried out in anguish, "My God, my God, why have you forsaken me?" (Matthew 27:46). By attacking the problem of evil which led to suffering,

He was dealing with the problem of pain at its root. On the cross God willingly carried the evils of the whole world. We shall never understand it. We can only marvel at His fantastic self-sacrifice. There God experienced the problem of evil more intensely than any human being could possibly know. And He did it to free us from the cancer of evil which had invaded our deepest being.

- Lastly, God has overcome the problem of pain and evil. He has solved it, not as a mental problem but in its capacity to overwhelm us. The cross, and the resurrection which followed, are the standing evidence that evil and suffering do not have the last word in God's world. There is hope. For the cross was not the place of defeat, but of victory (Colossians 2:13–15). On the first Good Friday Jesus died with a cry of triumph on His lips; triumph over pain and hatred, suffering and death, Satan and evil of every kind. And that first Easter Day He rose from the grip of death. Ever since then He has enjoyed the power of an endless life (Hebrews 12:2). Even death is a defeated foe.

And so the early Christians, and many of their successors ever since, have been able to see suffering not as an unmitigated evil, but as an opportunity to experience the victory of Jesus in their own lives. And that victory shed a light on the dark recesses of evil and pain, even when they could not understand them. The victory of Jesus rising from the tomb was for them a pledge of their own destiny from evil and from pain. They could safely leave Him to shed fuller light on it all in the life to come.

Christianity unashamedly looks beyond this life for the final solution of this mystery. But it does so confident that we have been given the key to the mystery in the cross and resurrection of Jesus Christ.

Christians believe in a suffering but overcoming God. And that belief prevents us from either becoming totally callous or going out of our minds at all the suffering which afflicts our world.

JESUS CHRIST WAS ONLY A GREAT MORAL TEACHER

Jesus of Nazareth is the most important figure the world has ever known. This Galilean peasant teacher has had more influence on mankind than any other person. We date our era by Him. Our educational system, our values, our standards, our laws, our medicine, and our love of justice and freedom owe more to Him than to any other source. Art, music, sculpture, thought, and literature have been more taken up with Jesus than with any other topic during the past two thousand years. Yet He is for all practical purposes ignored, except by a small minority. He is inconvenient. His very name makes us uncomfortable. And so He is condescendingly dismissed with a wave of the hand and the comment, "Jesus? Yes, of course, He was a great moral teacher."

Now undoubtedly He was a great moral teacher—one in a class of His own. He spoke with great authority: "You have heard it said, but I tell you. . ." He spoke with great simplicity, so that ordinary people could understand Him. He taught with remarkable depth: "Love your enemies and pray for those who persecute you" (Matthew 5:44) is a highly controversial and costly but exceedingly effective way of dealing with violent opposition. His wisdom silenced opponents time and again: "Give to Caesar what is Caesar's and to God what is God's" (Mark 12:17) has proved to be an utterly original and unanswerable bulwark against totalitarianism and also the guideline for Christians in public affairs. His teaching was embarrassingly specific and highly relevant to daily life: "Go and do likewise" (Luke 10:37) said Jesus at the conclusion of His most uncomfortable parable of the good Samaritan.

No wonder people marveled at the teaching of this man who lacked a higher education. No wonder they followed Him everywhere, hanging on His words. "No one ever taught like this," (see Luke 4:36) they said, and they were right.

But something else is remarkable about Jesus and His teaching. As well as teaching the highest standards known to mankind, He actually kept them. He not only taught people to love their enemies but also forgave those who crucified Him. He did not only call people to lay down their life for their friends but actually did it. He not only taught that it was blessed to be poor—He lived that way. It makes Him the most remarkable of all teachers. Here was one who taught the most exciting standards and actually embodied them.

Yes, Jesus was a great moral teacher. But neither He nor His followers will allow us to get away with the idea that He was that and no more. Jesus was either something very much more or very much less. He made the most astonishing claims, claims that have never been paralleled by any sane person. He claimed that He could forgive people's sins, that He had the right to people's worship, that He alone represented the way to God, the truth of God, and the life of God, that He had come to seek and save the lost, that He would give His life as a ransom for many, that He would rise from the dead, and that on the day of judgment humanity would be accountable to Him. (It is worth looking at the places in the Gospels where He says these things:

Mark 2:5; John 20:28, 14:6; Luke 19:10; Mark 10:45; Matthew 17:9, 7:21–25.)

To be sure, Jesus did not go around saying, "I am God." That would have been utterly misleading and totally incomprehensible. But, as Elton Trueblood put it, "All four Gospels bristle with supernatural claims on the part of Jesus. If He was only a teacher, He was a very misleading one." The claims came not only explicitly in verses such as those above but implicitly as He fulfilled prophecy, performed actions ascribed to God alone in the New Testament, and worked miracles. The claim to bring God Almighty into our world, to call people to God by calling them to Himself, confronts us on almost every page of the Gospels. It is part of the very fabric of the New Testament writings. It convinced some of the most determined and unshakeable monotheists in the world, Jews to a man. It convinced skeptics, political leaders, prostitutes, fishermen and tax collectors like the earliest disciples, and violent opponents like the brilliant and fanatical adversary Saul of Tarsus who became the most ardent believer. It has convinced billions of people all over the world ever since.

To say Jesus was simply a good moral teacher is untenable. It means ignoring half the evidence. If He is not the one who makes God real to us by sharing our human nature, He is either an untrustworthy liar or a deluded imbecile.

But why should we believe His claims? Many have made false claims for themselves. Many psychiatric hospitals contain deluded individuals. It is, and it ought to be, very difficult to think of Jesus as more than a man. And yet what are the alternatives?

- Was He a sham? But is it credible that this man who was so ruthless against hypocrisy should have built His whole ministry on a lie? Is it possible that He would have allowed Himself to be executed in the most excruciating of deaths for what He knew was untrue?
- Or was He simply mistaken? That will hardly do. If the greatest teacher of all is mistaken about the central issue of His life and claims, He is not such a great teacher after all. If we decline to credit what He has to say about His origin and authority, why should we pay any

attention to the rest of His teaching?

- Did Jesus perhaps suffer delusions of grandeur? Maybe this carpenter-teacher had ideas above His station, and His claims to deity were the results of some mental imbalance? That position is hard to substantiate. There are normally three key symptoms in those who are mentally ill. They have gross inadequacy in relating to the real world; they display gross inadequacy in personal relationships; and they are marked by gross inadequacy in communication. One has only to mention those three symptoms to see that they are each utterly inapplicable to Jesus, the supreme communicator, the man who possessed the most devastating insight into reality and was of all men the most loving and strong in personal relations. There is no trace of fanaticism or mental imbalance about Him.

Jesus of Nazareth was not simply a great moral teacher. He cuts too deep and steps out too far from the crowd for that. We can call Him a liar if we think we can sustain such a charge. We can cast doubts on His mental state. But the label of "only a great moral teacher" does not fit.

It was never an option in His own day. Some of His contemporaries thought Him mad; others loved Him. But He never seems to have received mild approval.

Neither is it an option for today. We have to shut Him up or hear Him out. The sheer impact of His person and His claims forces us to make up our minds. What are we to think of this great moral teacher who makes such impossible claims? Could He be right after all?

THERE IS NO EVIDENCE THAT JESUS CHRIST ROSE FROM THE DEAD

There is actually a great deal of evidence on this matter. There needs to be. Such an amazing claim ought not to be believed unless the evidence is overwhelming.

It is overwhelming! One erudite historian called the resurrection "The best attested fact in ancient history." Lord Chief Justice of England declared, "The evidence for the resurrection of Jesus Christ from the dead is so strong that no intelligent jury in the world would fail to bring in a verdict that the resurrection story is true."

Yet many close their minds to its possibility, let alone its truth. Some say, "Resurrections don't happen. They are against nature." But if there is a God who made everything and who is in control of this whole world, would it really be beyond Him to raise someone from the dead? Of course resurrections don't happen to every Tom, Dick, and Harry. Indeed, the Bible claims that the resurrection of Jesus is totally unique.

Nothing like it has ever happened before or since. He embodied the loving life of God in human flesh, and death, which is the last enemy for the rest of us, met its master in Him.

There is a tremendous sense of triumph in the New Testament accounts of Jesus' resurrection. "This man was handed over to you by God's set purpose and foreknowledge," said the apostle Peter in the very first Christian sermon, "and you, with the help of wicked men, put him to death by nailing him to the cross. But God raised him from the dead, freeing him from the agony of death, because it was impossible for death to keep its hold on him" (Acts 2:23–24).

So what the Bible claims about Jesus is not some resuscitation, like the kiss of life after drowning; not some temporary extra span of life which would end in death anyhow. But rather that in Jesus of Nazareth, and in Him alone, God's purpose for human life has been fully realized. After death He has been raised to a new quality, a new dimension of life. He is the first installment of what is intended for us all. He is the pledge of human destiny for all who trust in Him.

If it is true, this is the most amazing news the world has ever heard. It must mean that there is a God after all. It means that Jesus Christ really is His Son. It means that His death on the cross did not finish Him. On the contrary, He is alive, and it is possible to meet Him and be touched by His life and influence. If it is true, it means that we are not destined to go out like a light when we die, but that we are designed to know God and enjoy Him forever. It means that it is very important that we get to know Him now, while we can. It means that we need not fear death in the way we once did. The act of dying may be unpleasant, but it will be marvelous to be dead, for that is "to depart and be with Christ, which is better by far" (Philippians 1:23). So wrote Paul the apostle from prison as he himself faced the prospect of imminent death.

So the question of evidence is a very important one. A famous philosopher, Professor C.E.M. Joad, was once asked whom in past history he would most like to have met and what he would most like to have asked him. His reply: "I would most like to have met Jesus Christ, and I would have asked Him,

'Did you or did you not rise from the dead?' "
Well, did He? Five vital points indicate that
He did:

- Jesus really was dead. He was publicly
  executed before large crowds. He was
  certified as dead by both the centurion in
  charge of the execution and by the governor, Pilate, who sent to have the matter checked. Moreover, he had a spear
  pushed through His side just to make
  sure, and out came dark clot and pale
  serum, looking to the unsophisticated
  witness who records it like blood and
  water (John 19:34). There is no more
  certain legal-medical proof of death than
  that. Yes, Jesus was very dead that first
  Good Friday. The point would not be
  worth stressing were it not for the fact
  that some people, trying to evade the
  evidence for the resurrection, claim that
  Jesus was not really dead and revived in
  the cool of the tomb.
- The tomb was found empty. Jesus was
  buried in a new tomb, never before used,
  and therefore in mint condition and easily

recognized (John 19:41). But when His friends went to tend His body after the intervening Sabbath day, His body had gone; all the accounts agree on this. This was utterly astonishing. His enemies had been working for years to get Him dead and buried. So they made very sure of it and set a guard on the tomb and sealed an enormous boulder over it (Matthew 27:62–66). It made no difference. On Easter morning the tomb was empty. (It is worth reading the accounts, in Matthew 27:1–10; Mark 16:1–8; Luke 24:1–12; John 20:1–18; 1 Corinthians 15:1–11.)

That tomb was either emptied by men, or God did in fact raise Jesus His Son from the grave. But what men? You can discount his enemies. They were only too glad He was out of the way. Could His friends have removed the body? I think not. They were very discouraged and expected no such sequel to His death. And would they have succeeded in turning the ancient world upside down by proclaiming what they knew to be a lie, a lie for which they were content to be torn apart by lions in the arena? Read the story of the Acts of the Apostles, and ask yourself if it rings false or whether these people were utterly convinced of what they were saying.

• Jesus appeared after His death to many witnesses. The New Testament never places undue stress on the empty tomb. They were much more interested in the living Jesus who overcame their very legitimate doubts by appearing to them time and again—in a garden, on a walk, in an upstairs room, by a lake side. Each of the Gospels tells us about such appearances (which lasted only forty days, then ended as abruptly as they had begun). It is totally implausible to consider them hallucinations: They happened to hard-headed fishermen such as Peter as well as emotional women like Mary Magdalene, and civil servants such as Matthew. The resurrection appearances have never been satisfactorily explained away. They happened. And they demonstrate that Jesus is alive.

- The Christian Church owes its origin to the resurrection. Indeed, belief in the risen Christ was the first thing that distinguished the Christians from the other Jews. That belief brought the church into being swept through the Roman Empire. That belief lights up the hearts of approximately a third of the human race twenty centuries after the events in question. It simply will not go away. It grows and spreads into every nation under the sun. Why? If it is not true it should have faded by now, instead of expanding all over the world.
- Many, many people have encountered the living Jesus and have been changed by Him. It is not a matter of accepting one doctrine among many and defending it. It is a question of personal experience. All through the ages from the first century to this there have been literally millions of people, like Saul of Tarsus, who turned right around from being totally opposed or totally indifferent to Christianity to being utterly convinced it is true. What changed them? They met

with Jesus, alive, inviting them to respond in faith and challenging them to live His way. He changes people today, just as He changed the first disciples.

I have come to this life-changing encounter with Him. And it is open to anyone willing to look in the right place. Where is that? In the Gospels; examine the evidence there. Look into the Christian community at worship, and catch the flavor. Look into what you can take in of Jesus Christ and say, "Lord, if You are really alive, please make me sure of it. And then I am prepared to follow You wholeheartedly." Many a doubter has found that such a prayer is answered.

THE BIBLE IS UNRELIABLE AND CANNOT BE TRUSTED

The Bible is not a book at all. It is a library. It contains sixty-six books, written by an enormous variety of authors over a period of two thousand years in three languages. Some of the writers were Jews; some were not. Some were kings, some shepherds. The variety of literary genres in the Bible is kaleidoscopic: history and prophecy, psalms and poetry, Gospel and epistle, allegory and parable—even love story.

The really astonishing thing when you come to study the Bible is that, for all their diversity, the writers tell one story.

- You find the same view of God from the beginning of the Bible to the end. He is creator, savior, and judge. He is holy love.
- You find the same understanding of human nature: capable of the greatest heights of goodness and the greatest

depths of wickedness. Made to enjoy God but against Him, our supreme good is to be reconciled to God and to one another.

- You find a common view of Jesus Christ. He is both God and man. A real human being like us, He nevertheless brought into our gaze the God we could not otherwise understand. His death on the cross is not simply a supreme example of heroism. It shows on one hand the depths of human wickedness, determined to eliminate the best when we see it, and on the other hand the depths of God's love, willing to go to any lengths to rescue us from the alienation we had chosen. The Bible writers are clear, too, that on the cross something deeply significant happened: "He himself bore our sins in his body on the tree" (1 Peter 2:24). They are no less clear that death was not strong enough to hold Jesus. He rose from the tomb on the first Easter Day. He is alive today, and we can encounter Him. He can change our lives.

- You find the same hope. At the end of history God's purpose will be achieved on earth as it is in heaven.

There is no doubt that the biblical writers are united by the most astonishing harmony of outlook. I challenge anybody to find a parallel in history or literature in the world. Where else would you find such unity about God among so vast a disparity of writers across two millennia?

Comparative religion is a very interesting study, in which we find humanity in search of God and the different ends to that search. But the Bible is not really about humanity in search of God. It shows something much more surprising and radical: God in search of humanity. God is the supreme lover whom we have rejected, but He cares so much about us that He comes to find us, rebels though we are. There is no religion in the world that tells us anything comparable. But that theme, salvation, is the message of the Bible in its whole vast scope.

The Old Testament lies at the core of the three great monotheistic religions of the world: Judaism, Christianity, and Islam. It cannot be airily swept aside as "unreliable." It is one of the seminal works of all mankind. You cannot, of course, probe the truth of what it says about God. That is a faith judgment. But you can show that the transmission of its text is extraordinarily reliable. The Dead Sea Scrolls, found in 1947, give the Hebrew text of a number of Old Testament books. Written between 150 B.C. and A.D. 70, they are one thousand years older than any Hebrew manuscript of the Bible previously known. But the text is practically identical. It shows that we have extraordinarily reliable texts of the Old Testament.

And the Old Testament points beyond itself to a salvation which still lies in the future. As Augustine says so clearly, the New Testament lies concealed in the Old, and the Old is made clear in the New. And the centerpiece of the New Testament is Jesus Himself, a first century Jew who was executed under the Roman governor Pontius Pilate.

There is secular evidence for Jesus. Two of the famous Roman writers of the period tell us about Him, Tacitus (*Annals* 15.44) and Pliny the

Younger (*Letters* 10.96). So do Jewish writings, Josephus (especially *Antiquities* 18.3.3) and Mishnah. These texts attest His historicity, His unusual birth, His miracles, His teaching, His disciples, His messianic claims, His death by crucifixion, His resurrection, and His promised return at the end of history. There is also archaeological support, both that there were Christians and about what they believed, in the first century A.D., and also for the trustworthiness of Christian statements in the Gospels and Acts.

But of course the main source of information available to us about Jesus is to be found in the New Testament itself. Can we trust it? That boils down to three issues:

- Can we trust the documents? Do we have the New Testament as it was written, or has the text been tampered with over the ages?

The answer is that the text of the New Testament is so sure that nobody makes conjectural emendations for fear of being laughed out of court. We have so many manuscripts of the New Testament, written so near the events themselves, that we can be sure of having the correct text somewhere in the manuscript tradition—and the differences are not more than minor ones. No single doctrine hangs on a disputed reading. Indeed, there is no ancient book where the manuscript tradition is so early and so widespread as is the case with the New Testament.

As the celebrated biblical archaeologist Kathleen Kenyon wrote, "The interval between the date of the original composition and the earliest extent evidence becomes so small as to be negligible, and the last foundation for any doubt that the Scriptures have come down to us substantially as they were written has now been removed."

- Can we trust what the Gospels contain? It is one thing to have reliable manuscripts. It is quite another to have reliable material about Jesus.

Here again we can be very confident. The Gospels are not primarily history or biography or teaching: They represent a new literary form, "good news about Jesus." That good news was preached all over the Empire in the thirty years before Mark, the earliest Gospel, was written. Does that interval not give opportunity for corruption and invention to creep in? No. Professor C.H. Dodd, in one of the most influential books on the New Testament of this century, *The Apostolic Preaching and Its Development,* has shown that much the same pattern of preaching about Jesus can be found in all the independent strands that go to make up the New Testament witness to Jesus.

Some of the events written in the Gospels are open to external verification: In each case they come through with flying colors. But there are two tests which are particularly helpful to modern scholars. One is the test of Aramaic. When something in the Gospels can easily be translated from its Greek dress back into the underlying Aramaic which Jesus and His disciples used, it proves very reliable. The second criterion is multiple attestation. If some event or saying is attested by several strands in the Gospel there is a high presumption of accuracy. And that applies to central reports like the main teaching of Jesus, the miracle of the feeding of the five thousand, and Jesus' death and resurrection.

Although the subject of Gospel criticism is complex, it is true to say that no books in the world have been so minutely examined as the Gospels over two and a half centuries of scholarly criticism, and yet their credit stands today as high as ever.

- But what it really comes down to is this: Can we trust the person on whom the Bible concentrates, Jesus Christ? Does the account of His life and teaching, His death and resurrection, His love and challenge ring true? Is He someone whom we not only admire but desperately need?

Many who declare the Bible to be unreliable are very ignorant of its teaching. But they are very sure that they do not want to take the costly step of giving in to Jesus Christ of whom the Bible speaks. It is not what they can't believe in the Bible which is the trouble, as Huck Finn once said, it is what they can believe! That is quite enough to face us with a massive moral hurdle. If the Bible is true, are we going to receive its truth?

SCIENCE IS IN CONFLICT WITH CHRISTIAN FAITH

Top scientists do not make this claim, but ordinary people often do. For them science deals with facts, Christianity with values and emotions. Science can be proved, they say, while Christianity cannot. Science is progressive; Christianity has often opposed progress. The scientific method is logical; Christianity involves the leap of faith. Science deals with the laws of nature; Christianity, apparently, thrives on miracle. The contrasts are immense.

Immense they may appear, but they are myths all the same. Let's look at them one by one.

- Is it true that science deals with facts, Christianity with values and emotions? No. Both deal with evidence. Science deals with the evidence about our world which is presented by what we can see, touch, measure, and calculate. Christianity deals with what we can infer about our world from the life, teaching, death, and resurrection of Jesus. He is very much open to examination—by the science of history. His life and teaching, His death and resurrection are well attested. They are proper subjects for careful inquiry. The conclusions we reach will have far-reaching implications for how we see the world.

Certainly Christianity involves value judgments, but so does science. Both involve the agent as well as the object. Both have a subjective as well as an objective side. There is no such thing as an uninterpreted fact. Even emotions are common to both "scientists" and "Christian believers." Both are human beings. Both are reluctant to accept evidence which goes against what they have always believed.

The astronomer Robert Jastrow details the hurt and angry feelings of astronomer after astronomer at the implications of the Big Bang theory of cosmic origins. This now dominant theory parallels, in some ways, creation at some point in time and space—by a creator. And for some who have held out as unbelievers that is totally unacceptable. "It cannot really be true," writes Allan Sandage. "I would like to reject it," writes Phillip Morrison. "The notion of a beginning is repugnant to me," writes Eddington. Yes, science deals with values and emotions no less than Christianity.

- Then is it true that science can be proved, but Christianity cannot? Again, no. Science cannot be "proved." The heart of the scientific method is empiricism, allowing the evidence to lead you where it will. Very well, if that is so, it is obvious that you cannot prove any scientific hypothesis. It is a product of observed uniformities. But it would only require one contrary instance to bring the whole thing down. For centuries Newton's theories seemed to be proven, . . . then along came Einstein.

To prove a thing with certainty, you have to show that it follows inexorably from something already known. Only deductive knowledge is certain. Of course, for all practical purposes we accept the reliability of "laws" discovered by the sciences. But they are not proved.

Equally, you cannot prove Christianity. You cannot show there is someone greater than God from whom He can with certainty be deduced. That would be a contradiction in terms, for "God" is the name we give to the *ultimate* being. You cannot prove the historicity and teaching of Jesus Christ. You can't do it with Julius Caesar, either. Historical events are not "proved." They are accepted or not on the ground of competent, credible, and preferable contemporary testimony. That is the ground on which Christians ask acceptance of Jesus.

- Is science progressive, then, while Christianity opposes progress? There is some truth in that. But only some. "Christianity" has been opposed to progress at times in its history. You can think of the Orthodox Church in Tsarist Russia. Or of the Spanish Inquisition. Or of the church's opposition of Copernicus and Galileo at the dawn of scientific discovery.

But often Christianity has been in the van of progress. Progress in education, in medicine, in the liberation of the oppressed, of prisoners, of slaves, of women. And remember the many Christians involved at the start of modern science—Kepler, Priestley, Harvey. . .

Remember, too, the dark side of science. Think of nuclear fission—neutral in itself but opening the door to the destruction of the planet. Think of the terrifying possibilities opening up through biological engineering and chemical warfare. You might call these things "progress" in terms of strict academic science. But do they represent advance and progress for humanity itself?

- Well then, is the scientific method logical, while Christianity involves the leap of faith? That is another myth. There is, of course, a logic and an order in scientific enquiry; there is also an order and a logic in the philosophical, historical, ethical, and religious disciplines of Christianity. But as a matter of fact, both depend in the long run on faith. Faith is not believing what you know is not true, as one schoolboy defined it. Faith is self-commitment on the basis of evidence. And that is fundamental both to the scientific method and to the Christian faith.

You can't do without faith to begin either scientific study or Christian living. In both cases you need to commit yourself. In the case of science, you must commit yourself to the assumption that the world we see and touch is real, though there are grave problems in that assumption as every philosopher knows. You have to commit yourself to belief in the uniformity of nature and the prevalence of cause and effect. Without these prior "leaps of faith," reasonable though they are, you cannot begin science.

Equally, real Christianity involves commitment. Commitment to the assumption that there is a living God who has revealed Himself in Jesus Christ. Commitment in faith to Jesus Himself. Without that faith, that self-commitment on good evidence, there can be no Christianity.

In science, when you make a discovery, it is seldom by sheer thought or logic alone. There is that spark of imagination, that hunch, that experimentation. "What if I were to try this? . . ."

There you have it. Self-commitment—on

evidence. And if the experiment is successful you repeat it, and in due course it becomes an additional element in our knowledge. So it is with Christianity. The Christian claim is that God has not only made this world, but He has come to it. Christians then adopt the scientific method. They cannot know *a priori* if this claim is true. It is not a matter of sheer logic. They have to commit themselves to the hypothesis that it *could* be true and see if it *is*. They base their lives on the good evidence that certain things are true. Then they begin to discover that they *are* true: faith works.

Contrary to popular opinion, by far the greater number of those who are converted to Christianity in the universities are scientists. It is not all that surprising. The approach is so similar: self-commitment on evidence—or faith.

- And finally, what about miracle? If your theories are bounded by a closed physical universe with fixed and unalterable laws, you will find the concept of miracle, which involves the local and temporary suspension of those laws, intolerable. But that is a nineteenth century view of science, and you would find few scientists of stature supporting it. The whole scene is much more fluid since the discovery of quantum physics and Heisenberg's uncertainty principle. But the important point to remember is that "laws of nature" are not prescriptive, but descriptive. They do not determine what may happen; they describe what normally does happen. Science can say that miracles do not usually occur in the ordinary course of nature. But it cannot legitimately claim they are impossible. Such a claim lies outside the limits of science. And if God has really come to this world in the person of Jesus Christ, is it so very surprising that miracles were worked by Him, as the Gospels report? They cannot be ruled out as impossible. (They need to be carefully weighed for probability, but that is a very different matter.)

Science is not in conflict with the Christian faith. To be sure, some scientists are. Other scientists are passionately committed Christians, just like people in any other walk of life. The reasons for such decisions must be sought elsewhere than in science.

Inspirational Library

Beautiful purse/pocket-size editions of Christian classics bound in flexible leatherette. These books make thoughtful gifts for everyone on your list, including yourself!

When I'm on My Knees   The highly popular collection of devotional thoughts on prayer, especially for women.
    Flexible Leatherette $4.97

The Bible Promise Book   Over 1,000 promises from God's Word arranged by topic. What does God promise about matters like: Anger, Illness, Jealousy, Love, Money, Old Age, and Mercy? Find out in this book!
    Flexible Leatherette $3.97

Daily Wisdom for Women   A daily devotional for women seeking biblical wisdom to apply to their lives. Scripture taken from the New American Standard Version of the Bible.
    Flexible Leatherette $4.97

My Daily Prayer Journal   Each page is dated and features a Scripture verse and ample room for you to record your thoughts, prayers, and praises. One page for each day of the year.
    Flexible Leatherette $4.97

Available wherever books are sold.
Or order from:

Barbour Publishing, Inc.
P.O. Box 719
Uhrichsville, OH 44683
http://www.barbourbooks.com

If you order by mail, add $2.00 to your order for shipping.
Prices are subject to change without notice.